Colossians

Living as God's chosen people

by Helmut Harder

Faith and Life
Bible Studies

Faith and Life Press
Newton, Kansas

Therefore, as God's chosen people, holy and dearly loved, clothe yourselves with compassion, kindness, humility, gentleness and patience. Bear with each other and forgive whatever grievances you may have against one another. Forgive as the Lord forgave you. And over all these virtues put on love, which binds them all together in perfect unity

(Colossians 3:12-14, New International Version).

The publishers gratefully acknowledge the support and encouragement of the Congregational Resources Board of the Conference of Mennonites of Canada in the development of this book.

Design by John Hiebert
Printing by Mennonite Press, Inc.

Living as God's chosen people

Table of contents

Introduction

The Letter to the Colossians is a favorite book for students of the Bible. Its message is practical; its theology has depth; its style is personable. For these reasons, it offers the serious student an attractive Bible resource for inspirational Bible study.

This study guide offers the user a simple and straightforward way to study Colossians. The study process is designed to encourage a careful reading of the text and an application of the text to our time. The study guide can be used on an individual basis or in group Bible study.

The eight sessions in this book will guide you step by step through Colossians. In order to gain most from this study, follow the steps suggested below.

First, work through the study guide by yourself. Read through the assigned Bible passage several times, watching for special details, as well as for key words and ideas.

In getting acquainted with the passage, consider these questions:

- Why did the author write these words?
- What did the writer want to share?
- Why is this message important?
- What meaning do these words have for us today?

If you are working through this book with a group, write down your own answers to the questions before meeting with others. The more each person prepares ahead of time, the more fruitful your group study and discussion can be.

Encourage everyone in the group to take part. Be flexible and feel free to use this guide in whatever way benefits you and your group most.

The Bible text used in preparing this study has been the New International Version (NIV).

May this booklet lead you "to see Christ more clearly, to love him more dearly, and to follow him more nearly."

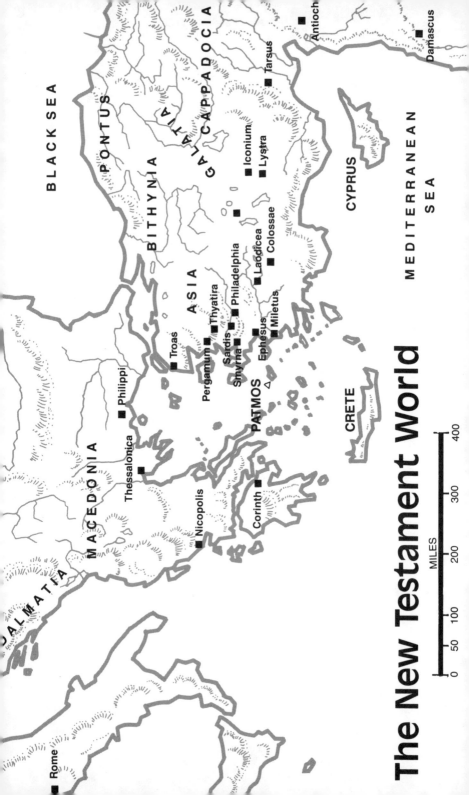

The New Testament World

Session 1. Grace and peace their greeting

Colossians 1:1-2

1. Read Colossians 1:1-2. Note every detail of this carefully stated introduction to the letter. How is the introduction different from the way we begin a letter in our day?

2. Are these verses similar to the way you would begin a letter to a relative or a dear friend?

A writer with authority
1. Fill in the missing information.

The letter to the Colossians is written by _____
(4:3; 4:10; 4:18). Most scholars say the writer is a prisoner

in _____ (See Acts 28.) at this time, but
may also have been at Ephesus or Caesarea. With this

person is a faithful co-worker, _____
According to 4:10-15, at least six other friends and faithful supporters are with the writer. They are:

2. At the beginning of the letter, Paul lists his credentials as a way of explaining his situation. Let there be no question about his authority. He is an _____ (firsthand messenger) of Jesus Christ; he has been called into service not of his own will, but by _____ Lest the Colossians worry about his suffering, Paul assures them that he can still (1:24) _____ and he can still _____ Christ (1:28). As though to prove to them that he is in good physical health, he assures them that he has written this greeting in _____ (4:18). He is sending the letter to Colosse with two men: _____ and _____ (4:7,9).

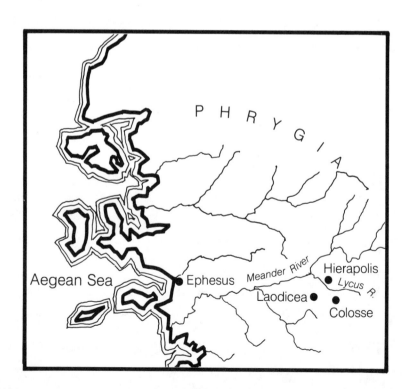

To the city by a river

1. Study the map. Scripture comes alive for us when we put geographical and historical wrappings on the text. Complete the following with the help of the map and the Scripture references: The city of Colosse, to which Tychicus and Onesimus carried the letter from Paul, belonged to the Roman province of _____ . Earlier

Paul had visited _____ , which lay

north of the _____ River, on the

_____ Sea. Colosse lay in the valley of the

_____ River, a tributary of the Meander River. Colosse was near two other cities in the area: twenty-one kilometers (13 miles) to the northeast was

_____ ;

and sixteen kilometers (10 miles) to the west was

_____ . (See 4:13, 15, 16.)

2. In New Testament times these cities lay on a much-traveled route between east and west.

The gospel of Christ was introduced to Colosse some years earlier, during the time that Paul was at Ephesus. (Read Acts 19:8-10.)

It is likely that Paul never went to Colosse himself at that time (2:1), but that he sent his missionary co-worker (1:7 4:12). Yet he felt a bond of Christian fellowship with the believers there. (See Col. 1:8; 4:8.) The date of Paul's Ephesian ministry is sometimes set at about A.D. 52 to 55. The date of his imprisonment at Rome, and thus the possible date on which the letter was sent, was about A.D. 60.

We will learn more about the writer, the people who received the letter, and the times in the following sessions.

Seven key words to know

The Letter to the Colossians is packed with important words. To understand and appreciate the message of the letter we will give special attention to some of these words. In the first two verses, seven words deserve special study: *apostle, will, holy, faithful, brothers, grace, and peace.*

Study the following notes, and then read the first two verses again, bearing in mind the depth of meaning that the Scriptures intend to convey in this simple introduction.

1. **Apostle**. This word means "a commissioned messenger" or "one who is sent." To be an apostle of Jesus Christ means to be sent by Jesus Christ. The word carries the idea of being authorized or having authority. In short, Paul writes to the Colossians under the authority of Jesus Christ. This gave the apostle great confidence to proclaim the gospel. It also has the effect of calling the Colossian believers to pay close attention to what is said.

2. **Will**. Paul's appeal to the will of God can be seen in two ways. Is he emphasizing that his authority is based on God's will and not on his own selfish will? Perhaps. Or, is he emphasizing, against those who had criticized him in Galatia, that he is not a second-generation messenger, but rather a firsthand evangelist of Christ? Perhaps. Both ideas have been suggested by Bible interpreters. In any case, Paul wants to make clear that his commission comes from God and not from a human source.

3. **Holy**. Some translations read *saints*, referring to a group of persons, rather than *holy*, a word to describe "brothers." Holy was used first in the Old Testament to refer to the people of Israel as a holy (consecrated) people. In the New Testament, the followers of Christ inherit this word.

What does it mean to be holy? It means to be consecrated or "set apart" for a special calling. The term *holy* says more about our dedication to a cause than about our past or present work and witness. In that sense, Paul can address Christians as saints even though they are not perfect. He respects their dedication to the Lord.

4. **Faithful**. This word has two sides to it. Faithful can mean that the Colossians believe in Christ; that is, that they are full of the knowledge of Christ. The term can also refer to the actions and emotions of the Colossians, namely that they are steadfastly faithful, that they will not deny their Lord even in hard times. But we need not decide between these two. They belong together. To believe and to be steadfast are inseparable. In any case, the mark of being faithful comes not from our own effort, but from God. God expresses God's faithfulness toward us in Jesus Christ. God's act of faith fills us with faith and binds us together in faithful community.

5. **Brothers**. The Bible was written in a society where males dominated in leadership positions. This was reflected in the church as well, even though there is some hint of an emerging female voice. Sometimes male language is used even though it is not meant to be exclusive, as in the case of Colossians 1:2. Surely Paul did not want to address only the men when he says, for example, that he is praying for them (1:9). Indeed, he sends special greetings "to Nympha and the church at her house" (4:15). Paul includes the holy and faithful sisters in his thoughts even though his words sometimes appear to exclude them.

6. **Grace**. This word is rich in meaning. It is often used in opening and closing greetings in the letters of the New Testament. By wishing grace for the Colossians, Paul is expressing the desire that the believers may enjoy the full experience of the mercy and goodness of God. The fulfillment of this wish for the Colossians will take at least a lifetime, since the experience of grace is meant to fill every part of life's experience now and to the end. Grace is not used only to describe the benefit of God to people. It is expressive as well of people-to-people relationships. To

live in grace is to forgive as we have been forgiven and to love as we have been loved by God. Paul's grace-wish to the Colossians contains a lifetime of good wishes and it is meant for every relationship.

7. **Peace.** Peace is a word that applies to every part of life. The Old Testament word for peace (*shalom*) applies to all of life: the personal relationships between people, international affairs, the land, the environment, the animals. The great aim of life is God's shalom. In the New Testament, Christ brings peace by his death on the cross (Rom. 5:1ff.). From the crucifixion flows inward peace (Phil. 4:7) and peace among humankind (Eph. 2). Thus, again, we can see that when Paul greets the Colossians with the blessing of peace, he has something in mind for them that includes every part of their life in this world. His wish is that in their life together they would live in the spirit of peace.

The writing and reading of letters

1. What personality and character traits do you sense in Paul as you read the opening verses of Colossians?

_____

_____

2. After reading these opening verses, how would you describe Paul's faith?

_____

_____

3. Letters I have received from believers in the Soviet Union often begin and end with a biblical greeting. What is the benefit of this practice?

_____

_____

4. Describe some ways in which we in our day could follow the example and spirit of Paul in the greeting that he addressed to the Colossian Christians.

_____

_____

_____

_____

One message in several parts

1. Now that we have been introduced to some of the background, we can proceed to the letter as a whole. Begin your study of the content of the Letter to the Colossians by reading the letter from beginning to end. This should take about ten minutes. Keep your mind constantly on the flow of thought as you read. When you have finished the reading, state the *central message* of the letter in your own words.

_____

_____

_____

_____

2. For our orderly study of Colossians, the letter has been divided into eight sections. These are shown in the chart below. Read the letter again, section by section. Write down a title or a central thought for each section.

TEXT   **MAIN THOUGHT**

1:1-2   Paul sends a warm greeting to the believers

1:3-14   _____

_____

_____

1:15-23   _____

_____

_____

1:24—2:5 _____

_____

_____

2:6-23 _____

_____

_____

3:1-17 _____

_____

_____

3:18—4:6 _____

_____

_____

4:7-18 _____

_____

_____

3. Complete the sentence: My personal goal in studying the Letter to the Colossians is

_____

_____

_____

4. In conclusion, share your goal with others and pray together that the Holy Spirit may guide you in the study of Colossians.

Session 2. Bearing fruit in every good work

Colossians 1:3-14

1. Now we begin our study of the body of the Letter to the Colossians. The text for this lesson can be divided into two paragraphs, verses 3 to 8 and verses 9 to 14. This division makes sense. Read the first verse of each of these paragraphs. Each verse refers to an activity of the writer's, namely:

2. This activity is mentioned again in verse 10. When we get to verse 12, we hear Paul inviting his readers to join with him in prayer, since the words "giving thanks to the Father" refer to the Colossians. Indeed, prayer describes well the mood of this text.

Much to be thankful for: 1:3-8
1. Into how many sentences does the Bible you are using divide these verses?

In the original Greek, verses 3 to 8 are one long sentence. Actually, it has only one main verb (*thank*), followed by a string of nine clauses held together by a variety of connecting words. The English translation has tried to simplify the rather complex original text. Read to verse 8, and see if you can find the nine separate clauses that follow the first eleven words in the NIV. Does this long sentence help you catch something of Paul's joy and enthusiasm? The original Greek reads like the lyrics of a moving hymn.

2. In ancient times, writers often began a letter with words of thanksgiving or praise. Non-Christian letter writers often began with the words: "Thanks be to the gods." Paul also begins with an expression of thanks (1:3) but he makes sure the readers know which God he means. How does he make this clear?

_____

_____

3. Becoming a Christian always requires a response in two directions, a double movement. How is this double movement stated in 1:4? Which two words in verse 4 express this?

_____

Which of these two parts of a full faith do you find more difficult to uphold in your life?

_____

4. Find three words in 1:5 that remind you of 1 Corinthians 13:13.

_____

Which of the three words provides the basis for the other two in 1:5?

_____

Someone has suggested that these three words uncover the richness of the scope of the gospel in that *faith* points to what God has done through Christ in the past, *love* calls us to express our devotion to Christ in the

_____ and *hope* points us to our assurance of God's victory in the _____ .

5. We often use the word *hope* quite easily. We say, "I hope so," meaning: "That would be nice if . . ." The Bible

uses the word in much greater depth. Hope is a word of confident assurance. Abraham organized his life of faith on the basis of hope in the promise that God would bless him with family and land. Job affirmed hope in the face of great suffering. The prophets held to hope in spite of Israel's sinfulness. The New Testament apostles faced life and death in the assurance that Jesus had died and risen. This gave them courage and power. Hope is much more than a strong wish or a heartfelt desire. Hope is built on the assurance of things to come.

Two further points need to be made about biblical hope. Hope does not focus merely on a reward at the end of life's journey. Hope focuses on a much larger event: on the final victory of God at the end of this age.

And, finally, hope should not allow us to escape from the present world and live only in the future with our thoughts and dreams. Hope is the driving force that calls us to be faithful in the present.

How does Paul's report in 1:6 strengthen the Christian's hope?

_____

_____

6. The final two verses of this paragraph (7,8) focus on Epaphras. Perhaps it was he who brought the gospel to the Colossians originally. In any case, he has come from Colosse to be with Paul. (See 4:12.) Paul calls him a fellow servant. The term _fellow_ can be understood as mutual: that is, a mutual servant to both Paul and to the Colossians.

Why did Epaphras come from Colosse? Two reasons might be suggested in these verses.

a. _____

_____

b. _____

_____

Tempted by a different gospel

7. To get the full benefit of this passage (3-8), we need to read between the lines. We might think that Paul is totally enthusiastic about these Christians and positive toward them. But he also has a deep concern on his heart.

Apparently, the believers had recently been tempted to follow a different gospel than the gospel that Epaphras brought to them. A hint of this appeared already in this paragraph. Some in the church were tempted to turn to the gods of the Greek religions; Paul says they have no other God than "the Father of our Lord Jesus Christ" (1:3). Some are inclined to turn to human notions in their search for truth; Paul calls their attention to the one "word of truth, the gospel" (1:5). Some are seeking religion in a sectarian and spiritualistic head trip; Paul says all you need is "God's grace in all its truth" which they learned from Epaphras (1:6, 7).

The Colossians need no new teachings. The teachings brought to them about Jesus Christ by Paul and Epaphras are enough. More will be said about this in later lessons.

Filled with the knowledge of God's will: 1:9-14

1. The prayer of thanksgiving (1:3-8) now changes to a prayer of requests. Verses 9 to 11 contain at least six requests for the Colossians for which Paul prays. List them here.

a. _____

b. _____

c. _____

d. _____

e. _____

f. _____

In the latter part of the paragraph, Paul calls the believers at Colosse to pray as well. He gives several reasons

(1:12-13) why they should offer thanksgiving to God. List these here.

a. _____

b. _____

c. _____

2. Notice the word *knowledge* in verses 9 and 10. Underline these words in your Bible. They provide a key to the message of these verses. In the original Greek, the root word for knowledge is *gnosis*. The word *gnosis* is also the root word for the name of a religious sect during New Testament times, the Gnostics. Paul surely has this sect and their influence upon the Colossian Christians in mind when he speaks here of knowledge. The Gnostics claimed to have a secret inner connection with God. They spoke of this as "spiritual wisdom" (v. 9). It had little to do with right conduct and had much to do with philosophical speculations.

Likely Paul has heard from Epaphras that Gnosticism is invading the Christian circle. So he wants to set them straight. At least three phrases used in verses 9 and 10 emphasize ethics or right living rather than lofty speculation as the key to a proper understanding of God. One of these is "the knowledge of his will." Can you find two others?

a. _____

b. _____

3. The biblical understanding of the Christian life is never static. It is dynamic and forward moving. The image of a pilgrim on the way to the celestial city comes to mind. In verse 11, two virtues or qualities of a Christian pilgrimage are named.

_____

_____

Endurance is a word used in battle to describe firm

resistance against the enemy. Thus the word calls the
Colossians to persevere in faith against false teachings.
At the same time, the word *patience* is an attitude which
we are called to use in relating to one another in the
community of faith. (See 1 Thess. 5:14.) The two words
give the faithful a two-sided defense and call them to a
balance between resistance and an unwearied love. Do
you find yourself in situations where the same advice fits?
Explain.

_____

_____

_____

An early Christian hymn

1. Edward Lohse, a Bible scholar, claims that with verse
12 we have the beginning of an early Christian hymn. He
says that the last word of verse 11, *joyfully*, should be
taken as a call to sing the hymn. The hymn then continues to verse 20. If that is so, we have here an example of
what is mentioned in 3:16: a spiritual song of gratitude.
You might try chanting or singing verses 12 to 14. It
works, even in English!

2. Verse 12 is one of the many places in the Bible where
redemption is spoken of in eschatological (end of this age)
terms. Which expression in particular emphasizes this?

_____

3. What two words in verse 13 tell us what God has
done for us?

_____

In one sense, we are rescued from "the dominion of
darkness," and in another sense we are not. Explain.

_____

_____

In one sense, we find ourselves in "the kingdom of the Son," and in another sense we do not. Explain.

_____

_____

Two meanings in forgiveness

Is the forgiveness of sins a one-time event? Or is it a continuing experience? It is one-time in that Christ died, once for all. When we claim Christ as our salvation, we have a one- time reference point, the death of Christ (Eph. 1:7). Our personal ownership of forgiveness has two parts: the leap of faith, whereby we claim, with assurance, that Christ died for us; and the constant and continuing appeal to Christ's offer of forgiveness in the daily experiences of ongoing life. The final victory over sin will come with the return of Christ and the full establishment of his eternal kingdom. Is the forgiveness of sins a one-time event or is it a continuing experience? It is both.

To conclude this session, share experiences of forgiveness. Think of where in your life and in your relationship with other people forgiveness is still needed.

Session 3. Christ—the image of the invisible God

Colossians 1:15-23

This passage has been acclaimed by students of the Bible as "the great Christology." The word *Christology* means "the word about Christ." This tells us that this passage sets forth a doctrine of Christ.

In Colossians 1:15-23, we find fifteen important claims about Christ. It may be confusing to try to count them, since something of the original sentence structure is lost in the translation from Greek to modern English. As you study the passage, let this great affirmation of Jesus Christ deepen your faith.

What is said about Christ in these verses is meant to be quite practical, yet is also quite lofty. The passage is an invitation to worship and adore Christ. Yet this great presentation of Christ has a real and practical purpose. Paul writes with a deep concern. He has the day-to-day life of the Colossian believers on his mind.

There's trouble in Colosse! And Paul wants to help the Christians "keep the faith" in the face of some real temptations.

We will begin by studying the great affirmations of faith in this passage. We will then move to its practical message for the Colossians and for us.

Firstborn over all creation: 1:15-23

1. This entire passage can be divided into two parts on the basis of who is talked about. The pronouns (I, you, and he, for example) at the beginning of verse 15 and at the beginning of verse 21 give the clue.

_____ and _____

Read each section (1:15-20 and 1:21-23) and write a title for each main thought. Begin your title with the personal pronouns you found.

1:15-20	1:21-23
He_____	_____
_____	_____
_____	_____

2. Notice that the first paragraph (15-20) divides into two parts. The first part (vv. 15-17) stresses the work of Christ in uniting the whole of

_____

The second part (vv. 18 to 20) focuses on Christ's role as

the _____

of all things in his work of reconciliation. The two parts are printed in parallel form below. Follow the instructions below the text.

1:15-17	1:18-20
¹⁵He is the image of the invisible God, the firstborn over all creation.	¹⁸He is the head of the body, the church; he is the beginning and the firstborn from among the dead, so that in everything he might have supremacy.
¹⁶For by him all things were created: things in heaven and on earth, visible and invisible, whether thrones or powers or rulers or authorities; all things were	¹⁹For God was pleased to have all his fullness dwell in him,

created by him and for him. ²⁰and through him to recon-
¹⁷He is before all things, and in him all things hold together.

²⁰and through him to recon-cile to himself all things on earth or things in heaven, by making peace through his blood, shed on the cross.

a. Circle all personal pronouns referring to Christ (for example, *he*).

b. Underline the words *image, God,* and *creation* on the left side and the words *head, body,* and *church* on the right side. Note that these groups of words set the tone for each part.

c. Christ is referred to in various ways in this passage. For example, as the *image* (v. 15). List the words that refer to Christ.

image, _____

_____

d. Draw a line from the reference to *firstborn* on the one side to *firstborn* on the other side. To which event does each refer?

_____

e. Place a square or rectangle around the words *all* and *everything* each time they occur. Now draw a line from each of these words to the word or words it refers to, for example: *all things.*

f. The word *things* is described more fully throughout the passage, usually with words linked by *and,* but not always. Circle these references (in color, if possible), for example: in heaven and on earth.

g. At three places in the passage, the main points are highlighted: at the ends of verses 17 and 18 and in verse 20. To whom do these words refer?

_____

What are the three key ideas (in your own words)?

a. _____

b. _____

c. _____

Holy in God's sight

3. The next paragraph (vv. 21-23) can be divided rather neatly into four parts. Each part contains a thought which leads to the next part. The following diagram makes the passage understandable. Write a title of a few words for each of the parts.

1:21	1:22	1:23a
_____	_____	_____
_____	_____	_____

1:23b

_____

_____

Now study the paragraph on the basis of the following questions:

a. Notice that the first three parts follow a time pattern. Using the words *past*, *present*, and *future*, give each of the three parts a time frame:

1:21   _____

1:22   _____

1:23a   _____

b. What does this observation about the time sequence tell us about our personal experience with the gospel?

_____

c. Notice that alienation (separation) from God (v. 21) includes references to both the mind and to behavior. Why does Paul link mind and behavior? Does one influence the other? Explain.

_____

_____

d. Notice in verse 22 that reconciliation is linked to both holiness ("to present you holy in his sight") and to forgiveness ("free from accusation"). Do you think Paul considers these of equal importance? Explain.

_____

_____

e. What clue does the _if_ part (1:23a) give us as to Paul's reason for writing the letter?

_____

_____

f. Which thought in 1:23b points us back to the first section of our text (1:15-20)?

_____

_____

g. Notice what Paul offers as his credentials (23b). He is

a _____ of the _____
What does this way of describing himself tell us about his personal character, his relationship to the Colossians and his convictions?

_____

_____

h. The second half of verse 23 probably provides a basis not only for verses 21 to 23a, but for verses 15 to 23a, and even for verses 3 to 23a. Read 1:4-6 again. Also, compare 1:23b with 1:7. Recall that Epaphras heard the gospel from Paul, and that the Colossians probably heard it from Epaphras.

All things reconciled

Read the following explanations. They provide background for understanding this passage.

This passage is an excellent reminder to us of the dimensions of the New Testament understanding of reconciliation or salvation. Being human and limited, even as believers, we sometimes limit our idea of where the saving work of God takes place. This passage brings home several truths about reconciliation.

First, God's work of reconciliation covers all of historical time. It took place in the past; it is taking place now; it will take place in the future. We should add to this that the plan of salvation was there even before past time began and that, finally, only a future eternity will reveal the full meaning of salvation.

Second, God's work of salvation relates to everything and to everyone. Note the reference to "all things" (1:20) and to "every creature under heaven" (1:23). We cannot claim that everything is already reconciled and that all people are already saved. However, we can speak of the powerful *potential* of the gospel.

Two practical things follow from this: missionary work and stewardship. The call to worldwide missionary activity is carried forward on the basis that the gospel is for everyone: for all creatures of God. The stewardship of all earthly resources is also a Christian calling based on the gospel of reconciliation since the "earth is the Lord's and fulness thereof" (Ps. 24:1, RSV). Truly, the gospel has wide application.

Faithful Christians must not despair if and when they do not see the fruits of their labor. It is hope (Col. 1:23) that keeps faith and works alive. In the end, the matter rests in the care of God, in whose power we are able to share in our place of work in the world.

Heresy at Colosse

Bible scholars are not completely certain of the exact nature of the false teachings against which this letter is addressed. The first century was plagued with many religious ideas and teachings. Some of these came from Jewish thought and some came from pagan religions. Both kinds are referred to in the Letter to the Colossians. In 1:15-23, it is the pagan religious beliefs that are being dealt with. Later, in chapter 2, we find clues that point to the influence of Judaism.

In order to understand our text, several important facts about the early church's experience need to be highlighted. The Greek religions and philosophies did not outrightly try to reject Christ. They wanted to include Christ into their religion. Christ should join their party of gods. Because of this, the New Testament church was always being tempted to make Christ something less than the Lord of all.

We see the answer to this temptation in our passage. Paul affirms the supremacy of Christ. Christ is not merely one of the many powers in the universe. He is *the* power of the universe. This argument leaps out from the pages of this text once we are aware of the problem that Paul is dealing with.

One specific religious teaching of the first century that has been identified is Gnosticism. It is clear that Paul has heard of the influence of the Gnostics in Colosse.

How do we know? Notice again the stress on creation in our passage. Paul says that God is the creator of heaven and earth; that "by him all things were created" (1:16). The Gnostics spoke against this belief. They believed that matter (the stuff of creation) is evil and that spirit alone is good. So God could not possibly have created things. This is, of course, a tempting thought, since we see so much evil and ignorance on the earth. Paul does not give in to this way of thinking. He does not write off the created order. Rather, he insists in keeping with the Scriptures:

God *is* the creator and Christ was active in creation as well.

Paul does not say that there is no evil on the earth. Rather, he speaks of the ministry of reconciliation which we must take up in the face of evil (1:20). The Christian cannot escape from the task of working in the midst of this earth for the sake of the reconciling gospel of Christ.

One final point needs to be made here. Notice the stress on the physical side of Christ's life. In 1:19, we read that "God was pleased to have all his fullness dwell in him." Verse 20 says that reconciliation was gained "by Christ's physical body through death." The Gnostics did not believe that the Son of God had appeared in a physical body. If physical matter is evil, they said, how could the Son of God have appeared in evil flesh and form. They completely removed Christ from the human sphere and thought of him as a kind of ghost or phantom. They said that when he walked he left no footprints.

It is against this false teaching that Paul speaks in this passage. How could Jesus Christ have reconciled us to God and helped us to become reconcilers in the world if he himself had not taken on human form? Of what use would the gospel be for daily life if the one who brought it to us had not created it in our very midst and in our lives?

Enough for now. More on heresies in later lessons.

Hope held out in the gospel

1. What does the message of reconciliation mean to you? How do you understand and apply the truth that God has reconciled "all things" to himself in Christ (1:20)?

---

2. How do you understand the claim that God has made "peace by the blood of the cross" (1:20)? How far does this message of peace apply? Peace with God? with people? in

the political realm? with all of creation?

_____

_____

Session 4. The word of God in its fullness

Colossians 1:24—2:5

In this passage, we catch a further glimpse of Paul's character. He refers to his joys and sufferings. He affirms his official commission from God. He expresses his compassion for the Colossians and his friendship with them.

But the passage gives us more than facts about the life of Paul. Rather, the text centers on two important related themes: Christ and Christ's body, the church.

Members of the body of Christ

1. Read the passage for this session.Count the number of times that *Christ* is mentioned. Underline them in your Bible.

2. Note every mention of the believers, the church. The word *church* does not occur as often. But remember that every reference to *you* is a reference to the congregation at Colosse and possibly also to the other groups in the Lycus Valley.

3. These two words, *Christ* and *church,* mean a great deal to Paul. He believes deeply in what we call the corporate nature of the gospel. The person of Christ finds expression in the body of Christ, the church. Christ is the head of the body, the church. To understand Christ, we must be united with Christ in the fellowship of the church. Paul thinks of himself not first as a lone individ-

ual, but as part of a community. It is vital that we recover
and promote this same emphasis in our day.

Delight and suffering

1. The entire passage is framed, at the beginning and at
the end, by a reference to joy and delight. What is Paul
joyful about (1:24)?

_____

   2. What does Paul delight in (2:5)?

_____

_____

   3. This passage has three references to suffering and to
struggle. Study these references, answering the two questions for each of the three texts.

Text	For whom is Paul suffering?	For what purpose is Paul suffering?
1:24	_____	_____
	_____	_____
1:28-29	_____	_____
	_____	_____
2:1-2	_____	_____
	_____	_____

Christ and Christ's body: 1:24-27

1. Paul links his suffering with the afflictions (suffering)
of Christ. He says that, in a way, the suffering of Christ is
not complete, and that he is making up for it. How would
you explain what Paul means here?

_____

_____

2. Here are some thoughts on the question you have just been pondering.

I am certain that Paul is not here raising a question about the completeness of the work of Christ for our salvation. Nor is he deciding in favor of gaining righteousness through works. Nor is he saying that he is equal to Christ in his suffering. This would contradict what has been written elsewhere in the New Testament. Then what does he mean?

One clue is found in the reference to the *body* of Christ, "which is the church" (v. 24). By linking Christ and Christ's body, the church, Paul is taking an idea from the Old Testament. Hebrew thought moves back and forth between the individual and the group. In fact, it does this so often that at times the two become one.

A good example of this is Isaiah 49:3 where we read: "You are my servant, Israel, in whom I will display my splendor." In this passage, a body of people, Israel, is addressed as an individual servant. The individual represents the community, Israel.

In the same way, the New Testament speaks, on the one hand, of Christ as an individual person; and, on the other hand, of Christ (his body) as a group of people. These two, the individual and the group, cannot be separated. What affects the individual affects the group, and what affects the group affects the individual. Paul, as part of the suffering church, belongs to the "body of Christ" which extends itself from the cross of Calvary to those on earth who devote themselves to the cause of Christ.

To understand the Bible on this point, we need to break with the highly individual way of thinking in our modern day. Community is more important than the individual; a relationship with Christ and Christ's body (the church) is central to finding faith.

Sharing in the suffering of Christ

1. Look up the following Scripture passages, and note what they tell us about sharing in the sufferings of Christ.

Mark 10:29 _____

_____

John 16:1-4 _____

_____

Acts 9:4 _____

_____

Philippians 3:8-14 _____

_____

2 Corinthians 4:10 _____

_____

2. We have seen how Paul explains suffering as an extension of the suffering of Christ (1:24). Sometimes Christians feel that suffering is a sign that God has forsaken them, or that they are being punished for some sin. How do you explain the suffering of God-fearing people?

_____

_____

_____

_____

Servant of the word of God

1. Paul continues to speak of himself in 1:25. He calls himself a servant. The original Greek word is *diakonos*. Which English word referring to a ministry in the church do we get from *diakonos?*

_____

2. Whose servant has Paul become? That is, to which word does *its* and *you* of verse 25 refer? (See v.24.)

_____

3. Verse 25 shows Paul with a place of responsibility in two directions: he is commissioned to present

_____

to _____

4. Which of the two is his authority?

_____

5. We are tempted at times to give people first place and to heed the word of God as an afterthought. Draw a sketch that illustrates the right way.

6. Which words describe "the word of God" in verses 26 and 27?

_____

7. Which expression in verse 27 further describes "the word"?

_____

_____

Mystery and the hope of glory

Notice the word *mystery* in verse 26. Are we to think of the gospel as a mystery? As something secret or hidden from some people? No. The gospel is public; that is, it is open for everyone to understand and to share.

Why then does Paul speak of it as a mystery? Because mystery was a word favored by the Gnostics. They had a secret religion, revealed only to a select few, understandable only to those who went through their initiation ceremonies. Actually, Paul will have none of this secrecy. So he emphasizes that the gospel of Christ has now been openly revealed, although he uses their word, *mystery,* quite often to make his point. (See also Rom. 16:25; 1 Cor. 13:2; Eph. 1:9; 5:32.)

Three verbs stress the fact that Paul has kept nothing secret. Can you find them?

In verse 25 _____

In verse 26 _____

In verse 27 _____

As he says in verse 27, Paul was especially chosen to make the mystery of the gospel known to the Gentiles. Being surrounded by their Greek religions and ideas, the Christians at Colosse would certainly understand his reference to mysteries.

With the energy of Christ: 1:28-29

The thoughts in these verses (1:28-29) hang on three references to Christ.

The first reference points to the message about Christ. What does Paul say about it?

_____

The second reference to Christ says something about the hearers of the message. In your own words, what is said about the hearers?

_____

The third reference to Christ says something about Paul's relation to the Lord. State this relationship in your own words.

_____

Truly, Paul was "a man in Christ," as the noted Scottish theologian, James Stewart, has said.

Full riches of complete understanding: 2:1-5
1. This paragraph begins (v. 1) and ends (v. 5) with a personal word from Paul. Between these is a twofold statement of Paul's purpose (vv. 2-3 and v. 4). Summarize or write a title for each of these four parts of the paragraph, using your own words.

Text   Summary or title

2:1   _____

        _____

2:2-3   _____

        _____

2:4   _____

        _____

2:5   _____

_____

2. It was a common practice to send the New Testament letters from church to church. Notice that a wider circle than Colosse is referred to in 2:1. Could the readers have included all groups in the Lycus River valley? Very likely, since a letter from the chief apostle would have produced great excitement among the believers and since there was a great deal of communication among the various groups. Do we have anything similar by way of intercongregational communication in our day? Where?

_____

_____

3. Paul names four goals for his readers (2:2-3). What
are they?

_____

_____

_____

4. These goals are probably addressed to the problems
that are bothering the Colossians. This becomes evident
from verse 4. Here we have Paul's first direct reference in
the letter to false teachings in the Colossian church.
What do you think is meant by "fine-sounding argu-
ments"?

_____

_____

5. Read verse 5 together with verse 1. The Greek word
for "struggling" in verse 1 is *agon* from which we get the
English word *agonizing*. This indicates an intense caring
for these Colossians whom he has never seen. It also hints
at Paul's knowledge that all is not well at Colosse. In
verse 5, Paul speaks appreciatively of how orderly and
firm they are in faith. How do you bring together this
positive attitude of verse 5 with the criticism that under-
lies verse 1?

_____

_____

6. To conclude this session, share your questions and
observations about the place of suffering in the Christian

life. What would you say to help another person see suffering from the Christian point of view?

_____

_____

_____

Session 5. Christ canceled the written code

Colossians 2:6-23

1. Read the text, and underline the name of Christ each time it occurs, as well as the pronouns (for example, *him*) that refer to Christ. In one sentence, state the main point this passage makes about Christ.

2. To understand the teaching about Christ in this passage, we must keep in mind that the gospel which Paul preached in Colosse and the other cities of Asia Minor did not drop into a vacuum. Religious worship of one kind or another was very popular in the Greek world. Their religions, with their devotion to many gods and goddesses, were widely practiced. In recent centuries, the religious traditions of the Jews with their rules and regulations had spread throughout the Greek world. More recently, the Roman state, with its emphasis on emperor worship, had made inroads into this area.

The most popular religion involved the worship of stars and planets. It was thought that one's personal future was written on the pathway of the stars. This religion appealed to people's sense of fate even as horoscopes have a following in our day.

The good news about the fullness of Christ came into this world. Some new believers replaced their former religion with an all-embracing belief in Christ. Others wanted to hold to their former beliefs and only add Christ to the other objects of their worship. But this does not work. Christ is all in all (2:9); he is the Head of the body (2:19). He is Lord of everything. There is only one Lord!

Are we faced with similar temptations in our day? How does this passage help us to find the right direction? (We will be discussing these questions in the course of this session.)

Built up in Christ: 2:6-7

1. Paul speaks in verse 6 of receiving Christ Jesus as *Lord*. What are some examples of Christian experiences you have had that give testimony to the lordship of Christ Jesus?

_____

_____

_____

2. How is receiving Jesus as *Lord* different than receiving Jesus as Savior?

_____

_____

_____

3. These two verses (6, 7) contain seven verbs (action words). Except for the seventh verb ("overflowing"), the others can be arranged in related pairs. Choose a verb that relates to each of the following:

received _____

rooted _____

taught _____

4. Notice the stress on both the foundation and the development of Christian faith and life. Do we give equal attention to both sides of the scheme as Paul does?

Not a captive of the deceptive: 2:8

1. As mentioned in earlier sessions, careful students of the Colossian letter say that a "Colossian heresy" was at work in the church at Colosse. In verse 8, we find three phrases which speak of this heresy. What are they?

_____

_____

_____

2. When you read verse 8, what comes to mind as to the nature of the heresy? How would you describe this false teaching? (Try this before you read the explanation under the next point!)

_____

_____

_____

3. Paul is not condemning the pursuit of philosophy (which simply means "love of wisdom") as such. Nor is he against all tradition. He is also not against basic principles, as we use that term today. Rather he has something quite specific in mind. Some in Colosse (even among the professing Christians) wanted to mix their faith in Christ with a cultural religion of that day. This religion was handed down ("human tradition") by very religious Greek philosophers. They held that the world (both physical and spiritual) is governed by a complicated system of spiritual powers ("basic principles of the world"). This system included levels of angels, the power of the stars, and mind-boggling ideas ("hollow and deceptive philosophy") of how all this fitted together. This system was thought to control one's every move and one's entire destiny in a mysterious way. Some in the church were trying to fit this system with God's revelation in Christ. Do we find anything like this to be a temptation in the church of our day? If so, where?

_____

_____

Raised by faith in the power of God: 2:9-15

1. In these verses, Paul answers the false teachings in two ways: 1) by a description of Jesus Christ, and 2) by a description of what Christ has done for the believer.

What is said about Christ?

(v. 9) _____

(v. 10) _____

What is said about the Christian?

(v. 10) _____

(v. 11) _____

(v. 12) _____

(v. 13) _____

What is said about God?

(v. 12) _____

(v. 13) _____

(v. 15) _____

_____

2. Find words (in vv. 9 and 10) that speak to the Colossian false teaching (mentioned in v. 8).

_____

(v. 9) (Remember that Greek religions seek to deny that God could be revealed in bodily form.)

_____

(v. 10) (The false teachers thought that something needed

to be added to Christ if God was to be fully known.)

---

3. Notice the phrase "power and authority" in verses 10 and 15. These words refer to spiritual forces which were thought to rule the life and thought of individuals and of society. In verses 12 and 15 we read of God's triumph over the powers and authorities. How was this victory accomplished?

---

4. Bible scholars point out that the false teaching at Colosse also included Jewish religious practices such as circumcision. We will read more about this in verses 16 to 23. Notice that verses 11 to 14 deal with circumcision. According to these verses, how should one understand Christian "circumcision"?

---

5. Referring to the resurrection of Christ, Paul says that believers are "raised with him through . . . faith in the power of God" (v. 12). Menno Simons liked to refer to Christian discipleship as "walking in the resurrection." Do you agree? Why? Or, why not?

Reality found in Christ: 2:16-23
1. This passage gives us more information on the false teachings at Colosse. List the words and groups of words that mention the heresy.

_____

_____

_____

_____

2 What evidence can you find in this passage that the false teaching may have been influenced somewhat by Jewish teachings?

_____

_____

3. Read Romans 14:1-12 and notice how that passage speaks to the same issue. Compare Colossians 2:16 with Romans 14:3-4. What is it that Paul is really criticizing here? the practices themselves? or, attitudes?

_____

4. And yet the practices themselves, such as celebrating festivals (Col. 2:16), abstaining from certain foods for religious reasons (2:20-22), and self-abasement (2:18) can be overdone to the point that they take the place of true faith in Christ. Verses 18 and 23 speak to the danger of overdoing certain religious traditions and habits. Is this a problem today for the individual Christian and in the church? Explain.

_____

_____

5. What did Jesus teach and do about the kinds of practices dealt with here? (See Matt. 6:16-18; 15:1-20; Mark 2:18-28; Mark 7:1- 23.)

_____

_____

6. Finally, it is not a question of whether certain practices and disciplines are right or wrong for a Christian. The question is whether we depend on these rituals and these acts as our chief means of nourishment and growth in our Christian lives. Our source for spiritual life is elsewhere. What do Colossians 2:17 and 19 say about this?

_____

_____

_____

Qualified for the prize
Another way to gain understanding of the situation in Colosse is to see whether we face similar issues in our day and to see how we and other Christians try to cope with these challenges. Talk this over with your study group. To prepare for this discussion, write out your answers to the following questions.

1. What temptations in our day pose problems similar to the false teachings at Colosse?

_____

_____

_____

2. What do we need in order to withstand these false teachings and to strengthen our Christian faith and walk?

_____

_____

_____

_____

Session 6. Living as God's chosen people

Colossians 3:1-17

Christians are called to holy living. This sounds simple, but it is not. We have all seen and tasted of the world, its attitudes and habits, its cultural and social patterns. In the world, we tend to follow natural desires. Sometimes this is not bad, but often it is. Natural desire translates quickly into selfishness, self-centeredness, materialism, and grasping for power. This happens because the world has no spiritual center strong enough to provide a guiding light for our words and deeds.

In contrast, we have Jesus Christ at the center. The passage we are about to study helps us to see how Jesus Christ can be a real help as we make our way through the maze of life. Christ's life, death, resurrection, present lordship, and future glory provide the key to our daily walk.

Read the passage. Note the introductory section (3:1-4) followed by two sets of guidelines, one focusing on negative acts (3:5-11) and the other pointing to positive practices (3:12-17). Note the contrast between "put to death" (3:5) and "clothe yourselves" (3:12). Someone has referred to Colossians 3:5-11 as the *put off* passage, and to verses 12-17 as the *put on* passage.

Life hidden with Christ in God: 3:1-4

In these verses, Paul shows that the life of the Christian is framed by the life of Christ. This truth is developed in a rather special way.

1. Who is the object of concern in these verses? That is, who is being talked to and about?

_____

2. How many times do the words *you* and *your* appear in these verses?

_____

3. Why does Paul speak to the community generally and not to specific persons?

_____

_____

4. Four things are said about the readers of the letter in these few verses. Two of these refer to the past, one to the present, and one points to the future of the believers. Find these items.

regarding the past

(v. 1) _____

(v. 3) _____

regarding the present (now)

(v. 3) _____

regarding the future

(v. 4) _____

5. Three events in the life of Christ are noted in these verses. Again one reference is to a past event, one is to something that Christ is doing now, and a third event refers to something that Christ will do in the future. Find these events.

an event in the past

(v. 1) _____

a present activity

(v. 1) _____

a future activity

(v. 4) _____

6. In this paragraph, the Colossians are given two instructions as to what they are to do. Find these and list them.

(v. 1) _____

_____

(v. 2) _____

_____

7. The readers are given two words of assurance. What are they?

(v. 3) _____

_____

(v. 4) _____

_____

8. What does the last part of verse 3 tell us about why Paul is writing the words of this paragraph to the church?

_____

_____

9. The phrase "not on earthly things" probably refers to both the *mind* (v. 2) and the *heart* (v. 1). What do you think is meant by heart as compared to mind in these verses?

_____

_____

_____

10. How do the thoughts of this passage express the idea that a Christian is someone who is "in Christ"?

_____

_____

_____

11. The reader of these verses could get the impression that a relationship with Christ calls us away from any concern at all with earthly affairs. Do you think this is really what is intended? How do you relate *heavenly* and *earthly* matters as a Christian?

_____

_____

_____

Putting off and putting on: 3:5-11
Since Christians have died to sin, they must become in actual fact (really) what they confess by faith (ideally). In this portion of Scripture, we can see the pull between the real and the ideal. We can also see what it takes to move in the right direction: a clear call to become Christlike.

1. This paragraph mentions the vices that are found in Colossian society, and apparently also still among some of the believers. There are two groups of five. List these.

In verse 5   **In verse 8**

_____   _____

_____   _____

_____   _____

_____   _____

_____   _____

2. Greed is idolatry, says verse 5. Explain.

_____

_____

3. Are the five sins listed in verse 5 all equally bad? Or, are some worse than others?

_____

_____

4. Look up Romans 8:13 and Galatians 5:24. These verses are similar to the thought in Colossians 3:5. For your record, copy these verses here.

Romans 8:13 _____

_____

_____

Galatians 5:24 _____

_____

_____

5. Explain what is meant by "Because of these, the wrath of God is coming" (3:6).

_____

_____

6. Verse 7 tells us that the Colossian Christians had come from the heathen world with its vices. The early Christian mission had called them out of this darkness into the light of Christ. Read 1 Corinthians 6:9-11 where we see that many of Paul's converts were reclaimed from an evil and pagan society. At the same time, Paul is dealing with people who were very intelligent. Their minds were often highly developed, yet their ethical standards had been very low. How does Paul's patience with these new Christians show itself?

_____

_____

7. Read verse 11 carefully. At first, it does not seem to fit the train of thought. How might the message of this

verse fit into the paragraph? (State your thoughts before reading the explanation.)

_____

_____

_____

8. The evils that beset the Colossians (and us!) have to do not only with *inner*-personal habits, but also with *inter*-personal evils. The Colossians lived in a society divided in many ways. Religious barriers kept Jews and Greeks apart; racial lines segregated the Greeks from all others; cultural standards came between barbarians (such as the Scythians) and the civilized Greeks and Romans; economic class cut slaves off from free men; sexual barriers separated male from female. These habits and attitudes were often brought into the Christian fellowship. Paul is talking about this dividedness in verse 11. In effect, he is calling for an attitude of love.

9. Read Galatians 3:26-29. Which phrases or ideas are similar to those in Colossians 3:11?

_____

_____

_____

10. What does the line, "but Christ is all, and in all" (v. 11) mean to you?

_____

_____

_____

Bound together in perfect unity: 3:12-17
Even though the NIV divides these verses into two paragraphs, they belong together. The *therefore* of verse 12 ties all the verses into one thought unit. This passage is read

often in the Christian church today. It is a beautiful and warm call to faith and love.

1. How does this passage provide a solution to the problems listed in verses 5 to 11, especially the problem in verse 11?

_____

_____

_____

2. List the virtues that you find in verses 12 to 15. There are about ten.

_____

_____

_____

_____

3. Circle the one virtue that is above all others: the one that says it all.

4. When we find it difficult to imagine how a person living on earth could be clothed with these attitudes, we are not left without an example. The example is named in verses 11 and 15.

_____

5. Look up the following texts, and copy them here, noting how they support the Colossian text.

John 13:15 _____

_____

_____

Romans 15:7 _____

_____

_____

Ephesians 4:32 _____

_____

6. How is verse 14 similar in emphasis to verse 11?

_____

_____

7. Notice that the call to peace begins with the heart and extends to the members of the body. Does it also extend to the groups of persons mentioned in verse 11? Does it extend beyond the members of the church? What is the answer to this question as given to us in the life (and suffering) of Jesus?

_____

_____

_____

8. List the three activities of the gathered church noted in verse 16.

_____

_____

_____

The second activity, admonishing, can refer to the task of the preacher and of brothers and sisters sharing mutual advice and encouragement with each other.

9. According to verse 16, what is the desired purpose for singing?

_____

10. Suggest some ways in which this purpose can be achieved more fully in the congregation than it sometimes is.

_____

_____

11. We sometimes speak and pray "in the name of the Lord Jesus" (v. 17). At times, we do this rather casually. Having studied the Colossian heresy we can see the crucial importance of doing everything, "whether in word or deed . . . through him." Explain the importance of praying "in the name of the Lord Jesus."

_____

_____

_____

The call to virtuous living

It is sometimes said that we live at a time in history when virtue is thought to be outdated, and "nothing is wrong anymore." The text we have just studied provides good direction and encouragement to Christians in the midst of today's society. It is impossible to think of Christian growth and witness without putting off evil ways and putting on the ways of Christ. Take some time to reflect on the call to virtuous living as taught in Colossians 3:1-17, and then write down your thoughts.

_____

_____

_____

_____

Session 7. Being watchful and thankful

Colossians 3:18—4:6

Just as the New Testament encourages us to relate our inner, spiritual life to our outer life, so also we connect our attitude toward one another in the church to the way we walk in the world. The Letter to the Colossians now turns to the matter of our relationships in the wider community. This includes the family and the work place. In other texts, such as Romans 13 and 1 Peter 2, the Christian's relationship to government is included as well.

1. Begin your study by reading Colossians 3:18—4:6. State one general impression that the text leaves with you.

_____

_____

2. This text follows a pattern. Outline the text under the following headings:

Text	Who is addressed?	Who is spoken about?
3:18	_____	_____
3:19	_____	_____
3:20	_____	_____
3:21	_____	_____

SESSION 7 / 51

3:22-25 _____ _____

4:1   _____ _____

3. Now group the persons addressed into three sets of two each.

_____ and _____

_____ and _____

_____ and _____

4. Notice how often reference is made to "the Lord" or "Master." Write every phrase that contains a reference to Christ. There are seven. The first one is done for you.

as is fitting in the Lord   _____

_____ _____

_____ _____

_____

5. What does this repeated emphasis upon Christ the Lord tell us about the main point of this passage?

_____

_____

Wives and husbands—be not harsh: 3:18-19
1. What advice is given to wives?

_____

_____

2. What advice is given to husbands?

_____

_____

3. Underline the main verb (action word) in each case. Is it a matter of husbands submitting to wives also? Or are wives only to be subject to their mates? (See Eph. 5:21.)

_____

_____

_____

4. Is the husband the *lord* of the wife? Must the wife always obey the husband? This passage is often under-stood in this way, but if we take the New Testament back-ground into account, a different interpretation and appli-cation of this passage is found. How do you interpret *submit to*?

_____

_____

5. The New Testament church found itself largely in a "man's world." It was assumed that men held the author-ity. Jesus had taught a different way: there is only one authority, God. Under God, all believers stand equally under the grace of the cross. This was the ideal, but the church also had to reckon with the reality of the social situation. For example, if wives became believers, but their husbands were not converted, the believing wife would need to exercise some patience and endurance in the home lest she anger the husband. To "submit to your husbands as is fitting in the Lord" (3:18) was a call to the wife to let love, patience, and peace guide her relationship as it guided Jesus' way to the cross. This explanation should not be used as a way of promoting male dominance in the family or in the church. The better way is to serve one another mutually in Christ.

On the basis of the above explanation, how might one interpret verse 19 (the word to husbands) in a case where the husband has become a believer but the wife has not?

_____

_____

Or, in a case where a society seems to tell husbands to manhandle their wives and treat them like material property, how does verse 19 apply?

_____

_____

_____

Compare Colossians 3:18-19 with the following passages: Ephesians 5:21-33; 1 Peter 3:1-7. Make one key observation.

_____

_____

_____

Children and fathers—not embittered: 3:20-21
1. When children are told to obey their parents in everything, does this really mean *everything*? Are there situations where a child cannot do so?

_____

_____

_____

Actually this wasn't really the question at Colosse. The word to children is spoken against a particular background. The Jewish influence was strong in the Colossian church. In the Jewish family, it was strongly emphasized that children should obey their parents without question (See Exod. 20:12: "Honor your father and your mother . . . .") This applied not only to small children, but to children of any age, even in the relationship to elderly parents. In the cultured homes of the Greek and Roman world of that day this was also the case.

But when persons became Christians, some tended to say (as we saw earlier in this letter), "We're free in Christ! We don't need to obey anyone!" We can imagine that some children would take this a step too far, and make a point of announcing their freedom in Christ and their loyalty to his lordship by outrightly challenging the authority of their parents, especially if the parents were not believers.

This had a twofold negative effect: It spoiled the Christian witness (You don't win people to Christ by making them angry!) and it disturbed the peace by creating bitterness between parents and children. So, what we have here is a call to "children" to endure a bit of suffering under the thumb of their parents for the sake of the gospel.

To get back to the question as to whether *everything* in verse 20 means everything: It can be assumed that children would not be asked, by Christ or Paul, to obey their parents if and when what is demanded goes against Christian principles. But in that case they should still not react with violence, but with long-suffering and peace.

2. Read 1 Peter 3:16-17. How do these verses relate to Colossians 3:18-21? _____

_____

_____

3. Notice that immediately after Paul says a word to children about parents, he says a word to parents about children (v. 21). Check several different translations of this verse (KJV, RSV, NEB, TEV, for example) and from these write synonyms for *embitter* and for *become discouraged.*

embitter _____

_____

become discouraged _____

_____

Paul is speaking to a problem that is still with us today.

Slaves and masters—serve Christ: 3:22—4:1

1. To whom are slaves finally responsible (v.24)?

_____

Who finally "pays" slaves?

_____

What difference should this make in their behavior?

_____

_____

  2. What does verse 25 mean?

_____

_____

   The point of this advice to slaves is to encourage them to show respect rather than disrespect to their masters, so that the true Lord will shine through their lives and their work. By the way, the word to slaves of the New Testament applies to all in our day who work under superiors or bosses.

  3. What are some words that mean the same as *right* and *fair* (4:1)? (Check various Bible translations.)

right _____

fair _____

   What is the reason given for calling masters to be right and fair?

_____

_____

Grace seasoned with salt: 4:2-6

1. Paul ends the main message of the letter with various instructions. This paragraph calls the believers to faithfulness in three areas of life. Read the paragraph carefully to discover these areas.

4:2-4 _____

4:5 _____

4:6 _____

2. Verses 2, 5, and 6 give specific advice to the Colossians. How does this advice fit the general situations described, especially the conditions touched on in Colossians 3:18—4:1?

_____

_____

_____

3. Paul makes a prayer request in his own behalf (4:3-4). His request has two parts. What are they?

(v. 3) _____

(v. 4) _____

The gospel of peace

The biblical gospel of peace is the foundation for Colossians 3:18—4:6. How are your personal life situations and your daily relationships affected by this gospel of peace?

_____

_____

_____

_____

Session 8. Faces and names for the family of faith

Colossians 4:7-18

We come to the conclusion of the Letter to the Colossians. The editors of the New International Version have entitled this section "Final Greetings." A careful reading of this text brings to light the depth of mutual support and fellowship that was present during Paul's time. It is amazing that in a day of no telephones, automobiles, or airplanes, the network of communication among persons could have been so close and warm.

In this text, Paul names no less than ten acquaintances. Some are with him in Rome. Others are in Colosse and the surrounding area.

Read the text and underline the name of each person mentioned.

Ten who were greeted
Gather information about each of the persons from this text and from related Scripture references. The information, when pieced together, forms a picture of the richness and breadth of the early Christian community.

1. *Tychicus*: 4:7-8
What three terms does Paul use to describe him?

His tasks _____

Information about Tychicus in other texts

Acts 20:4 _____

Ephesians 6:21 _____

2 Timothy 4:12 _____

Titus 3:12 _____
   2. *Onesimus*: 4:9
How does Paul describe him?

_____

His task _____
Information about Onesimus in other texts

Philemon 10-18 _____

_____

   3. *Aristarchus*: 4:10
How does Paul describe him?

_____

Information about Aristarchus in other texts

Acts 19:29 _____

Acts 20:4 _____

Acts 27:2 _____

Philemon 24 _____
   4. *Mark*: 4:10
How does Paul describe him?

_____

Information about Mark in other texts

Acts 12:12 _____

Acts 12:25 _____

Acts 15:37 _____

Acts 15:39 _____

2 Timothy 4:11 _____

Philemon 24 _____
   5. *Jesus (Justus)*: 4:11
How does Paul describe him?

_____

   6. *Epaphras*: 4:12-13
How does Paul describe him?

_____

His particular services

_____

Information about Epaphras in other texts

Colossians 1:7 _____

Philemon 23 _____
   7. *Luke*: 4:14
How does Paul describe him?

_____

Information about Luke in other texts

2 Timothy 4:11 _____

Philemon 24 _____
   8. *Demas*: 4:14
Information about Demas in other texts

Philemon 24 _____

2 Timothy 4:10 _____
   9. *Nympha*: 4:15
What are we told about her?

_____

10. *Archippus*: 4:17
What might we conclude about Archippus?

_____

Information about Archippus in other texts

Philemon 2 _____

11. List some things we learn about Paul from this long list of greetings that he gives.

_____

_____

_____

_____

12. What can you learn about the nature of the New Testament church from these many greetings? Name four traits of this church.

_____

_____

_____

_____

13. Which two towns are mentioned besides Colosse? (4:13)

_____ and _____

Find them again on the map on page VIII. One of these cities is named as one of the seven churches in the Book of Revelation (Rev. 1:11). Read Revelation 3:14-22.

14. What could the church in Nympha's house be like (4:15)? Is this possibly a "house church," separate from the main church at Laodicea?

_____

_____

15. What do the instructions in verse 16 tell us about what happened to apostolic letters in the early church?

_____

_____

The final autograph

1. Paul says that he writes the final greeting with his own hand (4:18). Does this mean that he did not write the body of the letter? Could a secretary have written the letter? Check this verse in the King James Version for an interesting additional note. Why do you think Paul adds the point that he is writing the greeting in his own hand?

_____

_____

2. Compare the last sentence of the letter, "Grace be with you," to the concluding words in other letters of Paul. Write the last sentence of the verses of the following texts.

Galatians 6:18 _____

_____

Ephesians 6:24 _____

_____

Philippians 4:23 _____

_____

1 Thessalonians 5:28 _____

_____

2 Thessalonians 3:18 _____

_____

1 Timothy 6:21 _____

Philemon 25 _____

_____

3. Which word is repeated in each of these greetings?

_____

4. In your own words, state what is the spiritual meaning of grace as a final greeting?

_____

_____

The Christian network

Think about the network of Christian support that surrounds your personal life. Think about the network of persons that promotes the mission of your congregation and of your denomination. How is it like Paul's situation? Have you experienced the strength of mutual support? How can the network be improved? Are there people in your circle of concern who do not benefit from mutual spiritual support at this time? Thank God for friends!

_____

_____

_____

_____

_____

Finally!

This brings us to the end of the Letter to the Colossians. May the rich message of this letter continue to surround and penetrate your life as you walk with Christ.

Books

Barclay, William. *The Letters to Philippians, Colossians, Thessalonians.* Edinburgh: Saint Andrews Press, 1959. (The Daily Bible Study Guide)

Caird, G. B. *Principalities and Powers.* London: Oxford Clarendon Press, 1956.

Guthrie, Donald. *Epistles from Prison.* New York and Nashville: Abingdon Press, 1964.

Hunter, Archibald M. *Galatians, Ephesians, Philippians, Colossians.* Richmond, Virginia: John Knox Press, 1959. (The Layman's Bible Commentary)

Johnston, G. "Letter to the Colossians," *The Interpreter's Dictionary of the Bible.* Vol.IV, 658-62. New York: Abingdon Press, 1962.

Lightfoot, J. B. *Saint Paul's Epistle to the Colossians and to Philemon.* Grand Rapids: Zondervan, 1879.

Martin, Ralph P. *Colossians and Ephesians.* Grand Rapids: Eerdmans, 1973. (New Century Bible Commentary)

Schweizer, Eduard. *The Epistles of Paul to the Colossians, to Philemon and to the Ephesians.* New York: Harper and Brothers, 1930. (The Moffatt New Testament Commentary)

Vaughan, Curtis. *Colossians and Philemon.* Grand Rapids: Zondervan, 1973.

White, R. E. O., "Colossians," *The Broadman Bible Commentary.* Vol. XI, 217-56. Nashville: Broadman Press, 1971.